STUFF THE BUSTARD

Stuff the Bustard

and other poems

by

the Bard of Bratton

Sue Kemp

THE HOBNOB PRESS

First published in the United Kingdom in 2020

by The Hobnob Press,
8 Lock Warehouse, Severn Road, Gloucester GL1 2GA
www.hobnobpress.co.uk

British Library Cataloguing in Publication Data
A catalogue record for this book is available from the British Library

ISBN 978-1-906978-81-5

Typeset in Adobe Garamond Pro 12/14 pt.
Typesetting and origination by John Chandler

*The cover design is based on a painting by Emma Edmondson, who works at
Pond Croft Workshops in Bratton*

Contents

Foreword

Sue has been our BBC Wiltshire Breakfast Show Bard for quite some time now. I can't imagine the show without her incredible talent!

She has an extraordinary mind. The speed at which she crafts her work is quite frankly ridiculous. Like one of those fabulous oriental chefs, Sue slices, chops and grinds each show's ingredients, gives them a good toss and a dressing, before presenting them on a dazzling radio plate.

Any subject goes: Football victories, cats on worktops, celebrities with ticks. Penguins in care homes, weight loss and hoovering your mattress.

Sue has a rare talent. I'm waiting for her first duff poem to drop into my inbox but I sense it's going to be a very long time coming!

Ben Prater
BBC Wiltshire

Preface

This book contains a selection of poems written for BBC Wiltshire's Breakfast radio show. All of the poems have been inspired by the good people of Wiltshire and their responses to various local and national events.

The subject matter of the poems is varied, but it would be fair to say, mainly feature 'little things.' Chips and hedgehogs and spoonfuls of sugar. A few tackle bigger subjects, like FIFA football and D-day and electric Mini cars.

Nearly all the poems in this book have been read live on air by Ben Prater, presenter of the Breakfast show to whom I owe huge thanks. Ben's encouragement has been unwavering, as has the generosity of Will Walder, producer of the show, in allowing air-time. Without the dynamic duo of Ben and Will, I doubt this book would exist. (So blame them!).

I would like to thank Martyn for his friendship and support. I would also like to thank John Chandler of Hobnob Press for agreeing to publish my book and for 'getting it done'.

I hope you enjoy reading this collection of poems.

Sue Kemp
February 2020

ANIMALS

How the animals all tried to teach Emma how to win Strictly

The Viscountess knew that the animals would
all wish to explain how her dancing steps should
be much like their own if she wanted to win.
And they called a big meeting and summoned her in.

'Keep your neck long' You can guess who said that.
'Land on your feet' That was said by a Cat.
'Cross the floor safely; our own tour de force'
advised Pelicans, Zebras, and Puffins, of course.

'Hold tight to your partner' Sloth said with a yawn
While 'Take dainty steps' was advised by the Faun.
'Be sssslinky' Snake hissed through flickering lips
'And remember to use, every bit of your hips'

All the animals stamped and whinnied and clapped.
And the Seal approved and its flippers it flapped.
'Safari so good' quacked mystical Duck,
'May your feet hear the music and we all wish you luck!'

How the dog's insurance hit the roof

Do check your policy document card
because insuring some rare breeds is hard.

Canary dog premiums! I just read a tweet
complaining insurance was too hard to meet.

And if your dog is a Johnson American bull
well, your bank account, oh, it will never be full.

Even a pit bull so sweetly called Erica
you cannot insure if it comes from America.

A Molosser, a Tosa, a 'blue nose' or 'red',
or anything else that with these has been bred,
no matter how cute it is when it's a weener,
it can grow to be huge if it's from Argentina.

If your dog is a Dogo; if it is at all 'Mastiff-y',
insurance is no-go, a total catastrophe.

But love it is strange! You must go with your gut
and God bless the bond between you and your mut!

In October 2018 Longleat Safari Park welcomed in 6 Australian koalas as part of a conservation programme.Sadly one of them, a female called Wilpena, had to be put down after becoming seriously ill. The park said it had no alternative after she developed kidney disease. Those that remained were the only Southern koala of their kind in Europe.

Longleat Koalas

I am a tree marsupial
And I cannot kick the habit
Of eating eucalyptus leaves.
Now if I was a rabbit
I'd eat more varied stuff,
But being a Koala well
I never get enough
Of chewy eucalyptus leaves.
It's so fragrant when you eat it.
The only side effect there is
Whilst it's taste is so terrific
Is it makes me sleepy most the time
Because its highly soporific.

The second koala poem celebrates the arrival, one year later, of a new male to liven things up! In October 2019 twelve-year-old Burke was flown from Osaka to the Wiltshire park to help boost its breeding programme . Originally from Melbourne, Burke flew in to England from Japan. This was at the time when the Rugby World cup was taking place. This is a short poem about his arrival.

The Koala that came in from Japan

The keepers that came with Koala
had been watching the rugby games live.
They enacted the great rugby passes,
while we waited for him to arrive.
Japan and Australia and England
combined in the fluffy chap's bod,
and his plane was onside when it touched down,
and the koala emerged from the scrum.
One keeper he passed the koala,
a late tackle, a pass and a ruck.
Then the Longleat Lads got a line break
and the koala was put on the truck!

Staff at a Wiltshire care home brought in two penguins named Charlie and Pringle from a breeding colony to interact with residents. It should be noted that penguins when trying to find a mate will stare at the penguin they like for long periods of time without moving. If the other penguin stares back a partnership is very likely!

The penguins that went to the care home

The folks sat in their care home
expectant on their chairs.
Two VIPs were on their way
both suave and debonnaire.
When they walked in, they gave a bow,
and their keeper also smiled
'I expect the last time you saw one of these
you were no more than a child?'
The penguins went around the room
then suddenly stood still.
One stood in front of Mavis.
One stood in front of Bill.
And they just stared at each of these,
completely still, unblinking,
and Mavis and Bill were mystified.
What were the penguins thinking?
'Oh Lord' the penguin's keeper said
'They're doing the penguin stare!
It's a common courting ritual.
Stay put upon your chair!
When penguins stand and stare at you
it means they think you're great
but... it also means they fancy you,
and want you for a mate!'
The penguins stared intently
and Bill and Mavis blushed

and refused to stare back at the birds,
and the penguins they looked crushed.
They waddled on around the room
resolved to be Platonic.
And Mavis held them in her heart
While Bill wrote down..... a mnemonic.

National Pi Day is observed annually on March 14th. The 3rd month and the 14th day of the year is a consistent day to celebrate the mathematical constant π. Also known as pi, the first three and most recognized digits are 3.14. National Pi Day is celebrated by pi enthusiasts and pie lovers alike!

On March 12, 2009, the U.S. House of Representatives passed a non-binding resolution (HRES 224) recognizing March 14 as National Pi Day.

Of course the way we write our dates is different to the US, but this did not stop a Wiltshire cafe from baking special pies for dogs on National Pi day!

Pies for dogs on Pi day 14th March

The waiter asked for each dogs choice
And each dog spoke in their own voice.
'I am a corgi and so I must
eat my pie with plain shortcrust.'
'I am a Pom, can't get enough
of pies with pastry that is puff.'
'Well, I can't move, I feel achey.
Give me the pie with pastry flakey '
'And I am a puppy who loves to chew
so give me pies made out of choux'

In December 2019 a very prickly situation was averted! Skippy the hedgehog narrowly escaped getting crushed when she was spotted on a Stevenage recycling centre conveyor belt after arriving in a skip.

Despite going through nearly all the recycling process, Skippy had no broken bones and was taken to a London care home to recover.

This poem combines Skippy's story with that of the Garbage cat who was found in a Wiltshire wheelie bin at about the same time.

Skip of the Skip

What's that you say?
   Skip's in the skip?
Skippy needs help! We gotta be quick!
Skippy the hedgehog is really in trouble!
Mixed up with the bricks and scooped up with the rubble!
She's on the conveyor all covered in dust!
We just gotta save her. We really must.
Now she's upside down in the tumbling machine!
With the rocks and the grit, but she's coming up clean.
Aw no! Here comes Martha the garbage cat!
She's jumped in too, face first, boom splat.
This is turning into quite a scene
with the cat and the hedgehog in the machine
rolling around like it's some fairground attraction.
Thank God someone's seen them and switched off the
     contraption.
They've both been saved! No wonder I'm lyrical
Because salvation for these was a true Christmas miracle!

Did you know that a whale's song reflects its social history and where it has been? Scientists discovered that whales 'swap songs' as they pass each other in the vast oceans. When they hear a new song they abandon their old one. Each whale is constantly attempting to sing in the language of their neighbours which they do with extraordinary brilliance showing amazing learning skills.

Song for a whale

I'm a great big whale
And I sing very whale
And I sing my brudders song too!
Cos we honk each udder
Yes we honk each udder
And we'll sing our songs for you!
We sing humpback, narwhal, sperm whale, grey
We sing bowhead, pilot, fin.
Cos we learn songs fast
from the whales we pass
With the bottlenose and minky too.

BBC Wiltshire's Breakfast Show presenter Ben Prater, and a team of helpers, pulled a giant inflatable Great Bustard bird around the county for Children in Need. They covered 50 miles in a five-day tour. People came and stuffed the bird with cash for the charity. And needless to say, stuffing the bustard really grabbed Wiltshire's attention. The whole campaign was called Stuff the Bustard and it inspired this poem...

Stuff the Bustard

I will say this just once which I hope is enough.
I am Stuff the Bustard, *my name... it is Stuff!*
But I'll tell you this, people, you've all got some nerve
chanting my *name* like it's some kind of *verb*.
Did you 'Champion' the Wonder Horse?
Or 'Rhubarb' the Cat?
Or 'Skippy' the Bush Kangaroo?
Course you didn't, but you are happy, happy as punch
to 'Stuff' the Bustard for something to do!
'Stuff the Bustard!' you cry like it's ever so funny
to thrust under my armpits your great wads of money.
I don't mind, for one week , since it's such a good cause,
and it's actually quite nice getting all this applause.
So, for Children in Need,
You can make me the fool
You can stuff the bustard
(but... don't muffin the mule!)

Some animals, birds in particular, are very good at getting worms to surface. They will stamp their feet or peck the ground to charm the worms up out into the open. Humans of course use different methods. Also called worm fiddling or worm grunting some people have made a living from this activity while others see it as a sport. In July 2019 the village of Harnham hosted a worm charming competition and some of the techniques used were rather bizarre.

Worm Charming

Tallest and longest and fattest of worms,
Worm Charming assembled his clan.
'They are approaching in great numbers'
he warned the worms 'But luckily I have a plan.
They will charm you, entice you, cajole you and poke.
They will use every trick in the book
To get you to surface in the heat of the day,
By wizardry, hook or by crook.
Resist them, my worm-folk, stay fast in the soil
And do not be tempted to move.
The threat it is temporary, and I am confident that,
After tea-time ,well, things should improve'.
Then the worms they were scared and they trembled and
      prayed,
And could feel the ground starting to shake
And the voices above, they were awful and proud
Like a crowd that was baying for blood.
'I'm using a method not seen for a while'
Said a man with a very slight lisp
'I will lure out the worms with this quill dipped in jam
and with flicks of this barbequed crisp'
And others were bragging of the ways they'd be using-
Cat o nine tails, and smoke bombs and drums,
electrodes and petrol and needles and tar,
and songs from the eighties (which was going too far!)

Yet the worms held their nerve underground.........
All...... but one.....For Little Skinny Ninny-Kins could
     hear the music play and he arose from out the soil and
     dreamily did sway.
No sooner had his head emerged than the paparazzi
     pounced.
There were cameras, flashing, Tupperware, and before he
     knew what, he was trounced! What became of Skinny
     Ninny-Kins? No -one really knows.He was sadly
     missed by all the clan,
and all his tiny holes. And the man who'd won by catching
     him?
What was his noble prize? A wiggly squiggly caramel chew,
strangely thin with dreamy eyes.

In March 2019, Armando the pigeon was sold at auction for £1.25 million pounds. The auction house called him the 'best Belgian long-distance pigeon of all time' and he was also dubbed the 'Lewis Hamilton of pigeons'.

The last three races of his career were the 2018 Ace Pigeon Championship, the 2019 Pigeon Olympiad and the Angoulême - and he won them all.

The champ, who turned five years old shortly after the auction, is now enjoying his retirement and has already fathered a number of chicks. What a great pigeon!

Armando the expensive pigeon

Armando the pigeon has many a fan.
A star from the egg where he first began.
They say that his egg had a halo of gold
and that when he hatched out he was totally bald.
But when feathers appeared, all surprisingly quick,
he could fly straightaway like a super fast chick.
The seed that he ate was the finest of grains
enhancing his feathers and giving him brains.
No plain common perch for this pigeon so dear.
In his coup there's red carpet and a small chandelier.
Toys made of flax and a mineral block
and his very own miniature grandfather clock.
He finds his way home from far far away,
and helps other pigeons make gold eggs to lay.

In December 2018, a poacher was ordered to watch the Disney film Bambi after he was convicted of illegally killing dozens of deer.

He was ordered to view the film at least once every month for a whole year.

It was reportedly one of the biggest poaching cases ever tried.

Bambi. The punishment

Judge gives poacher man a frown,
saying 'Guilty and you're going down.
The sentence harsh as harsh can be.
You're going down, to watch Bambi .'
The man he groans, his head in hands.
The court with one accord it stands.
They watch amazed as he is seized.
Saying 'Och! He disney look well pleased.'
Beseeching judge, the man confronts her,
'That is too hard. Why not Deer Hunter?'
'That wouldn't make you weep and mourn.
I've sentenced you to watch the fawn.'
The man then flinched. His eyes did run.
'I wish I'd never owned that gun.'

Putting the queen bee on a person's chin is a way of growing a bee beard. Worker bees gather round her and cover the lower part of the person's face. By this method travelling showmen and women will sometimes present themselves before a crowd wearing 'bee beards'.

It is an astonishing sight.

Bee beard

Step right up! Don't be afeard!
Your chance to wear a smart bee beard!
Roll up roll up and and come on in
And I'll put Queenie on your chin.
Before you know it you'll be clad
In the thickest beard you've ever had.
Cos the swarm will go where Queenie goes.
And it's only ever fatal if the Queen gets up your nose!

This next little poem is about a cargo of Space worms!

Their scientific name is Caenorhabditis elegans. They are only about 1 mm long.

Teams of scientists from Exeter, Nottingham and Lancaster universities hoped that experiments done with the tiny worms at zero gravity could lead to new treatments for muscular dystrophy.

When the launch of the SpaceX rocket was delayed for one day (after mouldy food was found on board), researchers worried the worms would be 'too old' for the experiments on the International Space Station (ISS). Consequently they prepared a 'back-up colony'.

These back up worms, however, were not needed. It was decided the original worms were not too old, being still in that delicate state of 'just turning into adults'.

This is the lament of the back-up worms who were denied a place on the NASA Kennedy Space Centre Space Shuttle in Cape Canaveral, Florida.

By the rivers of Florida

By the rivers of Florida
There we sat down
Yea-eh we wept
When we remembered Space X,
When the wicked
carried us away in captivity
Requiring of us a song
How can we sing our space song, now we can't go?
How can we sing our space song, now we can't go?

From around 1913 canaries were used to detect carbon monoxide in coalmines.

When the canary was distressed, the miners knew that conditions were unsafe.

The use of miners' canaries in British mines was phased out in 1986.

These days it is still possible to hear the phrase 'canary in a coal mine'. It is an expression used to refer to someone or something that serves as an early warning of a coming crisis.

This next poem is about air pollution.

Canary in the mine

Hear the canary in the mine!
It warbles when the air is fine.
But when it's silent, time to run.
Pollution surely has begun.
The canary! Silent now for years!
And we must listen to pollution fears.
Yea, for the dead canaries sake,
hear the changes we can take.
And let no-one say they've not been told
about Particles, Gases, Chemicals and Mould.

Catstration

The cats in the vets all lie in their beds
bemoaning the loss of their tractor treads.
'My chassis is gone!' says the Tabby from town.
The cats all wake up to see what's going down.
A Ginger cat spits, crying ' Something has changed!
My large undercarriage has been rearranged.
My owner has spent his disposable lolly
on an op to remove my detachable dolly!'
Though their landing gears gone,
and each cat feels sick,
they perk up when they realise
there is now less to lick.
'It's the end of an era. We are Cats Without Tackle!'
Then one cat me-owwed with a loud feline cackle.
'Our life, this day forth, will be Jeux Sans Frontiers!'
And the cats one by one agreed reasons to cheer!

Columbo's dog

There was Hacker T and Mutley,
Hong Kong Phooey too,
Toto from the Wizard of Oz
and also Scooby Doo
A hundred and one dalmations
And each one had a name
The greatest party ever
 For dogs of any fame
There was Pluto Snowy Jip and Fang
All had their own name tag
Except for one in the corner
Who alone was looking sad.
His name tag it was empty.
He just sat there drinking grog
'Columbo never named me.
He just always calls me 'Dog"
So the moral of this story,
if it doesn't sound too lame,
Is forget the bones and cookies
and just give your dog a name!

After sorting out some 2,700 sewer blockages due to fat, on 27th March 2019 Thames Water brought a massive 3D artificial fatberg to Swindon town centre. The idea was to highlight the problem of grease and fat in people drains.

In this poem the concept of fatberg and iceberg combine. The poem also reflects on excessive plastic and waste materials being dumped in our seas, and the effect on wildlife.

Fatberg

The polar bear looks quite aghast
at what he sees go floating past.
A berg it is, he's sure of that,
but not of ice. No, this one's fat!
The greasy mountain grey and hard
was huge, an Everest of lard.
Embedded in its oily mash
a multitude of human trash.
Cautious, Bear, he closer creeps.
Sees speed traps in unwanted heaps.
Ripped up parcels torn by dogs.
Wet-wipes, hairballs, spoons and clogs.
Then Bear observes the arctic action
of creatures drawn to this attraction.
While lemmings sniff a half flushed nappy
other creatures look quite happy.
There's Flabby Seal trying to steer!
Rambunctious fox cubs drinking beer!
While puffins swing on soapy ropes
the penguins slide down all its slopes,
'Our fatberg may not look so nice
but it's bigger than your one, Melting Ice!'
Bear sees they're right but stays aloof.
The world's gone mad, and here's the proof.

For the sake of foxey

For the sake of foxey
do not swear.
It hurts his pointy ears
and makes his bushy tail droop
and makes him shed wet tears.
So from the time that you awake
until you go to bed,
For fox sake, keep your language clean.
Clean thoughts be in your head.

Great Bustard

I wandered o'er the lonely Plain
wondering if the cloud would rain,
nibbling on my custard creams,
and engrossed with inward dreams.
When all at once I gave shriek,
withdrew the biscuit from my cheek .
For there, not but a foot away,
a wondrous bird in plumed array
staring at my biscuit hand
and taking somewhat of a stand.
Stamping, dancing on the grass!
A vision that I could not pass.
Silently I stood my ground,
astonished quite by what I'd found.
Conflicted by my love of custard
and admiration for the Bustard.

YOUTH

A level maths

Let's sing the song of A level maths
and celebrate your child's pass.
Let's mix it up with karaoke
in voices rapturous but quite croaky.
Flex daddy's brains and vocal muscles
juggling five round sprouts from Brussels
holding a cauliflower under each arm
ringing the bell on the brassica farm.
It's a function, a fraction
a happy mental tangle,
a mind dance, an action,
a cute and well drawn angle.
Carry one over and order a drink.
String vest theorists are brainier than you think.
A pass is a pass and you've passed the mental test
and we'll cheer you on
and wish you well
and send you all our best.

This may be a familiar scenario to some parents. A child astonished and dismayed his mother on 1st December by eating nearly all the advent calendar chocolates in one go. For whatever reason, the boy stopped the binge at number 21. He attempted to conceal his actions by pushing shut all the little calendar windows. He was caught in this fiddly task by his mother, who immediately rumbled his gluttonous deed. Nice try!

Advent Calendar Goblin

It's no good trying to cover your tracks
or papering hastily over the cracks.
It's no good, after you've gobbled the sweet,
closing the window; it will never look neat.
It's patently obvious what you have done.
You've gone right up to 21.
Why you stopped there I do not know.
But...I forgive you..now off you go.

The Apprentice

You're 21 today. You're 21 today.
When you fit the frame round the door
You'll never use nought but 2x4.
Your father says you can do what you like,
drive his car and use his bike.
So shout hip hip hooray.
You've done the course that no-one fails.
You've stuck it all with No More Nails.
You've finished your apprenticeship.
You start your job today!

Gooseberry

She is your humble furry friend
whose soul is kind and fair.
She watches while you have your dance,
while sitting on her chair.
She doesn't drink the alcohol.
She always has her phone
and always has the car keys
when you're ready to go home.
Everyone should have a Gooseberry.
A Gooseberry is cool.
They watch your back, and keep you safe.
And stop you being a fool.

Strictly Joe Sugg

Did you ever dream you'd go from Wiltshire roofer
to England's favourite rooky hoofer?
Why, they've likened you to Fred Astaire,
although you've now got redder hair!
Thatchers take their prickly chances
and you've stepped up for all these dances,
maintaining both your lines and poise
despite the raucous crowd and noise.
The costume department's frilly shirt
you wore and kept away from dirt.
You kept your actions free from scandal
like a white and upright candle.
You've kept your lips politely worded,
and your loins all tightly girded.
We'll honour you as best we can
saying 'Thatcher Joe, a Wiltshire Man!
Self-disciplined, hard-working,who,
helped raise the roof on Strictly nights,
and never climbed the ladder on his dancing partner's tights.'

14th December 2019 saw a Teddy bear toss at Swindon's ice rink. People threw their bears onto the rink which were later sold with proceeds going to Barnardos. At this time there was the 'wear your Christmas jumper to work day'. This poem combines both themes.

Threadbear

Bears came hurtling through the air
skidding 'cross the ice.
One broke its nose and cracked a rib
and bounced not once but twice.
But Threadbear wore his jumper
when he was taken to the rink.
And Boy gave Bear a cuddle
and a reassuring wink.
'We have to do it, Threadbear.
We have to face "the chuck".
But I'll keep hold of your jumper's thread
and I'll pull you back. Good luck!'
Boy breathed in deep. The Bear was chucked.
And through the air Bear travelled.
True to his word Boy held on tight
and Bear's jumper it unravelled .
Bear hit the ice, the jumper gone
Save but a single strand.
And he grabbed hold of the woolly thread
with his tiny furry hand.
Bear clung. Boy tugged
and hauled Bear back across the freezing ice.
But far from being traumatised
Bear found it rather nice!
'Oh you adrenalin junkie, Threadbear!
You've got excitement on the brain.
Good job I bought two jumpers
Now we can do it all again!'

'But this time Bear, I must let go.
For I am getting old.'
And Bear's eyes welled up
and suddenly the ice looked very cold.
'Another child will love you
and warm your broken heart
and when I chuck you this time
you must make a brand new start.'

,

What's terrifying the teenagers now?

We're not afraid of bogey men nor scared of any clown.
We only fear the broadband speed whenever it slows down.
There's villages, and roads where no-one ever goes
'cos if you ever go there your broadband speed *it slows*!
It slows! It's worse than creeping hell.
We cannot tweet or chat
We turn into sad zombies,
And you really don't want that!

The tick that bit Justin Beiber

When one creature bites another
infection goes two ways.
The tick gave Justin Lyme disease,
but developed a worrying phase.
For the tick it started *singing*
and it simply couldn't stop
as it crawled around the paddocks
with a hippetty-hippetty-hop.
'His songs they are contagious,'
the tick it did complain
'I've got all of his songs now
stuck firmly in me brain.'
The symptom that was prevalent
was a catchy Bieber hit
and the tick sang 'Never let you go'
every time it bit.

Willy's Wonky Ticket

Willy had been up all night
Scrolling every ticket site
Till he found the ticket of his desire
At a price considerably higher
Desperate he bought it and went along on the day
But was stopped at the gate by a man who did say
'This ticket is wonky. Don't act all surprised.
You know that the seller was not authorised.
This won't get you in, despite what you've been told.
'Cos a free ticket once given should never be sold'

FOOD

Barbie song

I like barbeques,
in my garden too-oo-oo
It's fun to light it, and ignite it.
You can cook pork chops
on charcoal in flip flo-o-ops!
Imagine eating, on outdoor seating.
Come on, Barbie
Cook the chicken
Oh-oh-oh-oh
I like barbeques
In my garden too-oo-oo
I get excited
When it's all lighted.
Chicken legs and wings
While everybody sing-ing -ings
In factor 50 we're feeling nifty
Come on Barbie
Cook the chicken
oh-oh-oh..
(and so on and so on *ad nauseam*)

This next poem is called Chips. Did you know that the first commercially available chips in the UK were sold by Mrs. 'Granny' Duce in one of the West Riding towns in 1854? In Scotland, chips were first sold in Dundee in the 1870s where it was described as the 'glory of British gastronomy.'

It is estimated that in the UK, 80% of households buy frozen chips each year. That's a lot of chips!

Chips

There's crinkle-cut, skinny, spread out on the bench.
There's rustic there's jacketed, duck fat and french.
There's thick-cut and oven, curly and straight.
Just tell me what chips do you like on your plate?

And how to eat chips? Again, much to be said.
Lined up side by side in two slices of bread?
Saucily drizzled with steaming hot curry
and grabbed from the chippy and scoffed in a hurry?
The subject of chips makes a tasty debate.
So tell me what chips do you like on your plate?

Horrible food

(can be read to the tune of ' My Favourite things')

Jellied moose noses
And unhatched boiled critters
Bright stinging nettles with grasshopper fritters
Stewed chicken toenails all tied up with strings
These are a few of my favorite things
Cream-colored ants eggs and crisp legs of spiders
Eyeballs and other balls
And shih-tzu with noodles
Mild cheese that's fried with some sphincters and wings
These are a few of my favorite things
Fermented herring and blue cheese with faggots
Sheeps lungs with suet and seasoned with maggots
Slippery mucus for stink bug hors d'oeuvres
These are a few of my favorite serves
Eat the dog meat!
Eat the bee stings!
When I'm feeling sad
I simply remember my favourite things
And then I don't feel so bad

The Laughing Cashier

I had one banana and chose the queue
where the checkout seemed near.
But alas, t'was the till with the laughing cashier.
Now the laughing cashier she is merry and good.
But she jokes all the time, way much more than she should.
The other cashiers they were dull, but got cracking.
The laughing cashier loves to chat while you're packing.
'Isn't it funny' she said ' when bags stick together?'
Laughingly blaming the change in the weather.
'We can't lick our fingers no more. We'll get done.'
And she carefully painstakingly rubbed with her thumb.
And slowly she peeled the white bags apart.
'There we are, that's the way. Now we can start.'
The customer in front then fumbling for coins
which set Laughing Cashier off, splitting her loins.
'Isn't it funny' she said ' when your card just won't swipe?'
And she laughed and she laughed while my banana turned
    ripe.

The astronaut that couldn't burp

'Who shall do the experiment about the fizzy drink?'
And Buzz he put his hand up though had no time to think.
So there he was high up in space
holding a glass right up to his face.
Now his team they had given him a stiff gin and tonic
and were waiting to see if the effects would be chronic.
For bubbles in space do not rise to the top
and fizzy drinks generally simply don't stop
with their fizzing and foaming. So drinking it?..well..
They wanted to see and be able to tell.
So when Buzz took a slurp of the fine fizzing gin
they watched for small signs of a change to his grin.
His chin first did wobble, then a twitch in his eye.
Then the bubbles in his stomach caused Buzz to cry
'Oh I feel I'm exploding' as out came the gas
from his nose, from his mouth, and from his astronaut ass.
His team duly noted the results of the test
and Buzz was applauded for doing his best.

The clump of dampness

The sugar bowl that I offered to him
had the sugar spoon in, and was full to the brim.
But there near the spoon for all to see
was a beige clump of dampness and a grain of coffee.
'What's THAT?!' he pointed, 'that isn't right!'
I said 'It's a granule of coffee. It's not going to bite'
He stared at the speck, at the clump, then at me.
'What if that coffee speck gets in my tea?'
I sighed, 'Just scoop around it. Give it a try'
But he looked very nervous as if he might cry.
'I can't tell how much sugar is in those clumps.
I think loose grains are lighter than big sugar lumps.
If that damp clump gets into my cup
My sugar intake might go up'.
'My dear, that's nonsense. All theoretic'
'Well we'll see about that if I go diabetic'
He grumbled and sipped. Same every day.
Then I plumped up his pillow, and tidied away.

Vegetable soup

(*based on 'My favourite Things'*)

Raindrops on parsnips and spuds on the pallet
Bright coloured carrots and warm beetroot salad
All kinds of roots that come tied up with strings
These are a few of my favorite things.
Cream-colored turnips and crisp garlic croutons
Burdock and cumin and onion with noodles
Hot greasy fries with a spoonful of sauce
These are the things in my favorite course.
Swedes in french dressing or jackets with butter.
Peanuts and earthnuts! I'm starting to splutter!
Polite crudites on a little side dish
These are the things of my suppertime wish.
When the veggies lose their flavour
When I'm feeling sad
I simply remember the vegetable soup
And then I don't feel so bad!

TRANSPORT

The Normandy landings were the landing operations on Tuesday, 6 June 1944 of the Allied invasion of Normandy during World War II. Often referred to as D-Day, it was the largest seaborne invasion in history.

The Landing craft were small watercraft, such as boats and barges, used to convey a landing force from the sea to the shore during an amphibious assault.

Because of the need to run up onto a suitable beach, the landing craft were flat-bottomed, often with a lowerable ramp, rather than a normal bow. This made them difficult to control and very uncomfortable in rough seas. Personnel on board were often sick.

This poem reflects.

D day landing crews

War well begun. Well underway. Well wishing for its Victory
    Day.
One prayer, one hope that you can savour
is 'War be free from any flavour'.
Then grab your rock-bun, leave your train.
No thought of top-gun in your brain.
And tight the feeling in your throat
when you first board the landing boat.
May homemade rock-bun
weight the lump that rises as you man the pump.
Oh swallow, swallow it, and pray.
God speed, God Speed the Victory Day.

BMW confirmed in the middle of 2019 that production of its new electric mini will start in Cowley with delivery of the first fully electric cars due in March 2020.

The state of the art automated Cowley plant has over 1,000 robots working on the assembly line.

This next poem is about someone wondering about getting one.

Electric minis

For a while now I've thought 'electric cars are good'
with engines somehow cotton fresh beneath their metal
     hood.
But in my mind the nagging thought
'They'd need a lot of charge'
because it seemed to me that on the whole electric cars were
     large.
But now they've bought a mini out
(and a mini is quite small)
I'm thinking that might charge real quick
And take no time at all.
Perhaps they'd charge up overnight.
Under electric rugs.
Which you can only do in cars that don't have sparking
     plugs.
And they're considerably less oily,
so need servicing less oftener,
So I could wash it with a doily
and a dab of fabric softener.
Yes I'd really love a mini
and I hope it's not a sin
To simply want a car that's clean
And easy to plug in.

This next poem was written after the Breakfast radio presenter described how thrilled he had felt finding an air pump still with credit on it. It was especially pleasing because the tyres of his car were desperately in need of a top up.

Garage joy

What seeks the man who needs inflation?
An air pump at a petrol station!
'Why here's an air pump that's still whirring!'
He cannot stop his heart from stirring.
Over his shoulder a glancing look,
takes the nozzle off its hook,
'Be still my beating heart! They'll hear!'
He wipes away a joyous tear.
His heart thumps most excitedly.
Oh YES! There *is* air, and it's free!
His celebration was a sight.
His celebration wholly right.
For the greatest wonder of this gifted puff
was…. it happened to be just enough!
Now the cosmos, aye, when it was new
began with a gift of free air too.
The big bang was a kiss fond blown
as believers believe and scientists have known.
If on your travels anywhere
you find some gift of useful air
remember just from whom it came
and celebrate it just the same.
By the grace of it we all do live.
Thanks, free air, for what you give.

Oh your car's too big

The little Panda next to him
was relatively small and slim
so he thought he'd get his side door open.
leastways that's what he was hopin'.

A thud brings someone running back.
'You've hit my car you idiot!
You dinged my Panda. See this scuff!'
'It's the spaces .They're not big enough!'
'You should've bought a smaller car.
Your car's too big, too big by far.'
'If you moved your little Panda over
there'd be more room for my Land Rover.'
'Then I'd be on a yellow line
and I would have to pay a fine!'
'I'll pay your fine. Just move your car!'
'No , your car's too big, too big by far'

The trailer that ran away

The garage door was easy.
An up and over cinch.
The itchy footed trailer
didn't even need a winch.
No sooner had the flap swung up
than the trailer it rolled out
and gazed in glee at the open road
to see who was about.
Look right,
look left ,
look right again.
It slowly crossed the lane.
The trailer was a runaway
with freedom on its brain.
That happened several months ago.
Step forward now in time
and see it in this present day
all caked in mould and slime.
What happened to you, Trailer?
What awful things befell?
Your mirrors have gone cloudy
and you really don't look well.
Slumped, off kilter, scuffed and bruised,
unloved, alone, unhitched.
In a layby that is crescent shaped,
the trailer lies unpitched.
Had they been mistreating you?
Or were you just headstrong?
It's sad your bid for freedom
has gone so badly wrong.

The parking poem

To reverse or not to reverse?
That is the question.
Whether tis safer from behind, to mutter
n wing-mirrors, 'bout angles, and the supermarket's own
outrageous fortunes,
Or take your chance front first against a sea of drivers,
And, whilst opposing them, park up- and let the engine die!
To park, and by 'to park' to say we end
The journey; the needless starts and stops
That traffic daily bears. 'Tis polluting!
Devoutly we'd unwish the fumes to seep!
Small chance, small beep, perchance to brake, avoid the rub!
For in that bumper contact what dreams do come
of compensation
for cars already scuffed and dripping oil?
Just let us pause.
What should we say,
Or rather 'pay', in car parks?
Our coins? Nay! 'Tis respect,
lest, disrespecting others,
Going this way that way this way that way,
our own car ends up wrecked.

SPORT

Don't play croquet if you can't see the hoops

(the salutary tale of poor John)

Poor John tripped over the croquet mallet
when he slipped on his lawn in the snow.
He trapped his foot inside a hoop.
It was a tragic way to go.

With cheek upon the frozen slush,
and croquet jumper soaked,
while freezing icicles formed round,
the croquet player ... croaked

England's bid to reach its first Football World Cup final since 1966 came to an agonising end on 7th July 2018 when they lost in extra time to Croatia in Moscow. Croatia scored the winning goal in the 109th minute of the semi-final. England players were inconsolable at the final whistle. The dream snatched away at the last. This poem was written ahead of the game, when all the nation were intensely hopeful for England to bring home the Cup.

FIFA World Cup 2018

On Russian soil the fans await
with flags of their own nation.
Excitement binds them all as one,
the English and Croatian.
One wind unfurls the English flag and helps the other fly;
Each used on the opponent's face to gently wipe tears dry.
For football is a heartfelt game, and victors still must care.
To stand in victory's glorious state,
Believe, and Do, and Dare!
Go tackle, tackle, tackle hard. Dance sweetly like a lamb.
Go leap and swerve around like gnats,
Go head it like a ram.
And goalie, oh sweet goalie, dive with arms like octopii
And be the team that wins the match.
We know that you will try.
Whatever Croats throw at us, whatever Croats do,
whatever ref or Var man says, we're England fans, and true.
So lace ya boots ya Croat lads. Go lace them England, too.
Should England beat you, Croats, well, we will not crow at
        you!
Believe it! Be this English game!
Fe-fi FIFA fo fum!
For we can smell the victory
on the boots of the Englishman!

In January 2019 a new word was created....Firling!
A portmanteau word combining fir tree and hurling intentioned to serve as a verb for the sport of throwing Christmas trees.

The first ever Firling even took place on 5th January 2020 in Bratton Wiltshire. The event drew the attention of local media, got on page 2 of the Telegraph, and even was filmed for the local news on BBC!

All who took part where encouraged to shout out 'I firl ye fair fir' and firling the tree signalled the spreading of good wishes and good will to all men. This poem suggests ways to firl.

Firling techniques

You can swing it round in circles.
You can throw it like a dart.
You can take a good long run up.
You can stand with legs apart.
You can shut your eyes and make a wish
and take a big deep breath.
You can shrug it off your shoulder.
You can get it off your chest.
You can grunt, you can yodel,
throw it straight or let it curl.
With a good warm wind behind you
you can do a cracking firl.
You can grip it by the fairy end
or grasp it by the trunk.
You can firl it while you're sober.
You can firl it while you're drunk.
If you hurl your fir tree further
than the other folk can throw
you can win the Golden Fir Cone.
So grab your fir and have a go!

Mindful, *or* The effect of Japan on the England Team

Before this final game is played
a word now for the hosts
who, despite a typhoon,
kept intact the pitches and the posts
and catered for the nations
with delightful green tea brews,
extractor fans and sushi
and stunning Temple views.

Here now on the pitch we stand,
where our gumshields taste like steel.
God knows we need our anthem song
for this final test is real.
There is a mass of waving flags,
loud chanting from the throng.
The Springboks may act lively
but their gumshield's are biltong.

They say life is a journey.
A learning time for all.
We've already learnt to play the game,
and we've learnt to pass the ball.
We are mindful of our own skills,
mindful of our chums,
mindful as we run the pitch,
and mindful in the scrums.

Whatever outcome this game has
the journey is unbeaten.
And we have stories now to tell
of things we've seen, and eaten.
We play best when our pulses race.

We are powerful and fast.
We call the game ' Who'll outstrip Who?'
Or 'Who will be outclassed?'
(Post script)
Come, wrap us in kimonos
Now this rugby game is done.
And let the team reflect awhile
In the Land of the Rising Sun.

The Punter

The punter loves his racing days.
Gets dressed up and always prays.
He knows he is an outright sinner
but hopes one day he'll back a winner.
Now the various ways he chooses names
are rather wacky and quite strange.
One day he let his hamster walk
across the racecard dragging chalk
and where the chalk mark drew a line
the punter cried out 'That one's mine!'
Another day he scattered names
into a fire full of flames
and from the ash withdrew a cinder
'This is the horse that none will hinder!'
But the method which caused most annoyance
was when he tried to use clairvoyance,
for he could not see the horse that stays,
only the error of his ways.

This next poem arose at the end of May 2018 following the extraordinary enthusiasm shown by hundreds of Wiltshire folk for BBC Wiltshire's Step into Summer challenge.

Not only did they collectively smash the 100,000 mile target but they reported all the usual health benefits associated with regular walking: weight loss, fitness, and sense of well-being.

Many people across the age groups used the Step-o-meters issued by BBC Wiltshire. They began counting all their daily steps and contributed by phoning, emailing or texting in their amounts to the Breakfast programme which converted the steps to miles to boost the total.

This poem was a celebration of Step into Summer's success.

Step into summer

Well we trekked in V-necked T's,
and we've bared our knobbly knees,
and we've ambled, scrambled, wandered, pondered,
burning calories.
Step counting all the time.
Doing more than thirty-nine.
'Cos we'd filch a few from our neighbours who
said 'Wiltshire can have mine!'
And we've come so far,
and we've done so well
and we never stepped in anything
so far as we can tell.
We're just glad all our amounts
show Wiltshire really counts.
Yes we're glad all our amounts
Show Wiltshire really counts.

Swim

Backstroke, breaststroke, butterfly and crawl.
Nose clip, face mask, rubber hat and all.
Back flip, high dive, belly flop in style.
One length two length, swim a mile.
One mile two mile three mile four
River Thames, round Britain, cross channel more
Blond hair green hair in a speedo suit
Protein milk shakes lots of fruit
Train hard, keep fit, eat well, swim
Flex those joints now in the gym
All that power. Slow it down.
Fresh foot powder, dressing gown.

Women's Fifa semi-final

Look now upon the Lyon crowd,
as the England flag unfurls,
and bright star spangled banners
are held high by wonder-girls.
This is a first class battle ground.
We're the Lionesses fans!
And we're cheering for the underdogs
to beat the Ameri-cans.
If we win we'll dance the can-can
and we'll leap about and chant.
And if we lose we'll do the same,
and not say 'Ameri-can't.'
We call it 'semee-finals'
Americans say 'sem-eye'.
It doesn't matter how you say it
We know both teams will try.
So let your pony-tails down, girls,
but keep your boots laced up.
For what lies beyond this Lyon match
could decide the whole world cup.

NATURE AND THE ELEMENTS

You know it's autumn when

You know its autumn when
the lawn in the morning glistens
and you gaze lovingly upon the moist grass!
For Autumn is awe-time
and delights in our wonder.
Truly you know it's autumn
when you
give dew
care and attention.

Heatwave

I saw a moving staircase
And on one of its steps
A small thermometer.
I said to the man
What is that?
He said
It's escalating temperatures.
I saw the flickering flames of a fire
Like hands going side to side.
I said to the man
What is that?
Heatwave. He said.
I saw a young boy smooth his mother's arm.
What's that?
Sunstroke.
And so it went on
Day after day
And it wasn't funny at all.

The lunar eclipse

'What shall I quote you', says the Moon,
'for the services I have done for you
and the wrongs you have done to me ?
I have balanced your axial tilt,
lit up your nights and measured your months,
ebbed and flowed your tides.
It is time I was paid.
I've been jumped over by cows,
and howled at by wolves,
I've worn that Wee Willie Winkie hat
that made me look a prat.
I have hung in your space while asteroids
bypass you and stick in my face.
I've been like a fly paper in your room,
attracting your flies.
It is time I was paid.
You have disrespected me;
raked the reflection of my face
from ponds, crying 'Cheese, cheese!'
deliberately to tease.
You blame me for the madness
of your drunk pranksters
who go mooning out of cars
and make me the butt of their jokes.
But they will never contemplate the stars as I do.
So settle your debt and we will be one.
Send me sunsets for one night
so I can bathe in sun's light
and sup on the blood of the Sun.

Rule of Thumb

This knowledge from the radio!
It's like a wondrous gift!
It told me how we all could tell
when all the fog would lift.
'The eight month's fog doth lift at eight'
'The ninth month fog by nine'
'The tenth by ten' et cetera
With the promise all be fine.
In January it is 12 less one.
Go steady, let's not hex it.
For Rule of Thumb serves England fair,
Yea, with or without Brexit!

Snow

Some people don't like snow.
They are prejudiced against
water droplets that are below a certain temperature
that freeze into little fluffy shapes.
And they use 'snowflake' as a derogatory term.
These people are snowist.
They are too proud to walk like a penguin
and they lack imagination to build things
like igloos, and snowmen.
They are thermal wussies
to whom snow angels are anathema.
They stay in.
But those who go out
join the church of the playful,
shout greetings across to strangers,
build and slide and roll around like puppies
ecstatic on the equal ground.

Too hot

The sunshine is showing up my dusty shelves.
I know they're not going to clean themselves.
I've got the can of polish and the yellow cloth.
But do I feel like doing it?
I do not, because the room's too hot!

Dandelions are growing in my flower beds.
All the other flowers now have dropped their heads.
I've got the wheelbarrow and the trusty hoe.
But do I feel like weeding them?
No no no because the ground's too dry!

The dog is looking anxious, needs a you know what.
She knows that she's on carpet so she cannot squat.
I've got my sonic whistle and extending lead.
But do I feel like walking her?
No indeed, because the sun's too hot!
That's right, I said the sun's too hot!

Windy

Whenever it had blown a gale
Tom would grab his plastic pail.
He'd go outdoors and love to find
the things the wind had left behind.
Once he found a shopping trolley
and a child's action dolly,
some pages from the radio times,
and things that once had been wind chimes,
some lids blown off his neighbour's box
and keys blown out of someone's locks,
bottles rolling down the streets
and wrappers from some chocolate treats.
A mat, a hat, a cat, a plait,
(Who would've thought of finding that?)
He'd blink the water from his eyes
each time he found some random prize,
and grew quite rich but stayed a loner
'cos he'd sell each thing back to its owner.

HOUSES AND HOMES

The graveyard house

There's a family moved into our graveyard
and it's weird because they are alive!
We weren't told by our graveyard committee
but we'll be there when they arrive.
They are spooky these real-life people!
They wander about in the day.
They don't wail and moan like we do
They just worry about what they should say.
They worry about what clothes to put on
and what they will eat and then drink.
Living people are right proper weirdos.
Much scarier than you might think.

Home for abandoned Smart Phones

The home for abandoned smart phones
was a sad, sad place to see.
Phones with no cases shivered and moaned.
But one seemed different to me.
'What about that one?' I said, 'That one there.
Can I take out it for a talk?'
The phone it shuddered in my hand and gave a muffled
     squawk.
'There's no history with that one' the attendant lady said
'At first when it came in we thought that it was dead.
Remember now phones are for life! Don't take one on a
     whim!'
'I understand, I really do'
'Alright. I'll get its sim.'
She slipped the sim into the little phone
and its screen lit up all bright.
'Come on, let's get you home' I said,
'You're going to be alright.'

The hospital bag

Because it had been sudden, I'd had no time to pack.
My husband very kindly put some things inside a bag.
Thoughtful. 'You'll need some slippers.' And so I felt assured
that there would be the things I need while I was being
        cured.

In hospital Nurse asked me if I had brought a dressing gown
and I reached into the bag he'd packed..but something made
        me frown.
My fingers they detected ...an... unexpected feather!
And there was silky cloth and shockingly...
something that felt like leather!
I smiled nervously at Nurse, but my pulse was racing higher.
I said 'My hubbie means well,'
as I put on my attire.
Then all the patients, Sister too, erupted into laughter
Cos when I'd dressed in what he'd packed, I could not have
        looked much dafter.
A motorcycle jacket and a flimsy camisole
A pair of monster slippers and a fluorescent peacock stole.

The house in the Crematorium

I am not going to say anything jokey.
There's not much that needs to be said.
Our house does *not* get all smokey
just because there is somebody dead.

Though we live by the big crematorium
on a site where the dead bodies burn,
the incinerator's very efficient,
when the ashes to ashes return.

True, the location's not everyone's cuppa,
and we don't live in an architect's gem.
Still that chimney it billows life stories
and our house is 'The crème de la Crem'.

The new build that you build

This is the new build that you build.
It will stand up to light summer showers.
It's flat pack and comes with instructions.
You can call it your own Fawlty Towers.
Don't worry at all if you're unskilled.
There's this glue from a tube that you squeeze.
The walls hold together by suction.
But once inside it we advise you 'don't sneeze'.

To the mattresses

An Englishman's home is his mattress.
He'll keep it most beautifully clean.
He'll vacuum and spray it and beat it
to keep it all fit for his Queen.

He'll vacuum the surface for toast crumbs.
He'll bang it to raise up the dust.
He'll turn it and top it and tail it.
A clean mattress is simply a must.

No dust mites disturb his sweet slumber.
It is never allowed to get specked.
He'll hermetically cover the surface
with a sheet specially made to protect.

The trainer that moved onto a wall

There was an old lady who lived in a shoe.
She had so many children she didn't know what to do.
When the children grew up they had to leave home.
They had to go out find a shoe of their own.
So if you lose a shoe and are in a bad mood
it's probably been taken by one of her brood.
Now some shoes are too smelly to move in straight away
and they'll leave them on top of a wall.
It's not they don't like it and don't want it for home.
It just needs an airing that's all.
For the old woman's children are many indeed
and if you find that you've lost a good shoe
remember that homes are in such short supply
And say 'Please take the other one too!'

MISCELLANY

British

What is a British person, or if you will, a Brit?
What unique special qualities combine
to make the label fit?
Well here's the top ten list of quirks,
though it's not at all exclusive
belonging to our character
both eccentric and reclusive.
Apologise for everything whenever you are slighted.
Insist the future's far away and deny that you're short sighted.
Eat absolutely anything that's put before you on a plate,
accepting all life's ups and downs and call it simply fate.
At weddings sing the Gloria. At funerals Survivor.
And always smile whilst driving up behind a learner driver.
Stand in line most patiently in the supermarket queue,
and place customer divider bars between other customers
      and you.

Coins

I went to throw coins in the fountain
I thought that it might bring me luck.
But when I leaned forward to do it
my sleeve in the fountain rim stuck.
It ripped half the cuff off my jacket
and a button fell in with a splash.
Never reckoned on such an ordeal
to simply dispose of my cash.
When I looked in the depths of the fountain
I saw buttons from other folks coats.
I saw five p's and one shiney sixpence
and what looked like commemorative groats.
There were fifty pence pieces for Brexit
that nobody wanted to trade.
When people threw them in the fountain
I wonder what wishes were made.

Kemp and Hewitt's mill in Trowbridge produced over 300 miles of blue grey cloth for army uniforms.

Service personnel from Britain, France, Serbia and Japan all wore uniforms made of Trowbridge cloth. Even an American, one General Pershing, wore a uniform of this highly regarded material.

This next poem, written during Wiltshire Armed Forces Day celebrations, reflects on cloth as a blend of different threads and equates that with the Army itself being a blend of personnel and skills.

Consider the cloth

Consider the cloth in which soldiers are dressed
and which covers the backs of our fighters and crew.
It's a mixture of fibres, in the collar, in the sleeve.
It is rarely pure cotton on its own in the weave.
When they go out to fight, when they go to defend,
they go forth in a fabric best described as a 'blend'.

It's a blend, like their teams are.
It's a blend, like their skill.
The Armed Forces complexion is much like its twill.

Though they pay with their lives, and they go when we send,
when a uniform's ripped it's most tearful to mend.
As they step out in service we all pay for defence,
since no uniform's made at the wearer's expense.
Yes we're proud of the forces, and we own what they do,
and we'll wave the fine flag that is red, white and blue.

Here's a weird story!

    An Australian widow, Michelle Bourke, decided to travel the world with a life size cardboard cut-out of her late husband.

    Michelle travelled for three years, carefully taking Paul with her on trains and buses and ships and planes. When she and Paul came to Wiltshire in May 2019 there was much interest. They visited Bath and Stonehenge. Michelle said that she had fulfilled the promise they had made with each other when they were young, that they would one day travel the world together.

Cut out Paul

Her loved one, Paul, she'll not forget,
Not with his cut-out silhouette
standing in the lounge or hall
where he looks much thinner and quite tall.
Yes, a cut-out of the one she lost,
which is colour fast and nicely glossed,
has helped her through a time that's hard.
'My husband Paul was such a card'

How colour you this County?

'How colour you this County, Maid?' the traveller said to
      me,
'If Wiltshire was a colour, pray, what would that colour be?'

'Why the colour of a bustard, Sir' I answered to the Squire,
'The handsomest of colours, Sir, a colour to admire.'

'Extract me such a colour from this bird of which you speak,
and give it me in tincture form. From a plume mind! Not its
      beak.'

So I found a plume upon the Plain and boiled it a while
and its colour, like the very land, seeped out, and made me
      smile.

Hard to define, the colour was part compost and part stone,
and laborious were my efforts to describe the distilled tone.

I rolled my words like hills around and the Squire was
      enthralled
but threw me quite, the moment when, he asked me
'*What's it called?*'

'What called?' I said in panic. Then in somewhat of a rush,
'Why, Sir, this glorious colour of Wiltshire's land,
is known as... Bustards Flush!'

I did it myself

When the fuse blew on the plug
and the mower cut out
I did not scream. I did not shout.
I went to the shed with the cobwebby shelf
got a screwdriver down, and I did it myself

When the wallpaper peeled
and looked really bad
I did not start crying. I did not feel sad.
I went to the shed with the cobwebby shelf
got a packet of glue, and I did it myself.

When the house needed fixing
and things started falling
I did not phone builders. I did not start calling
I went to the shed with the cobwebby shelf
and gave a big sigh, and climbed on it myself!

Jack Lurke

Jack Lurke would do no work
His wife was just as lazy
Their children shirked
And never toiled
Which drove the neighbours crazy.
But Jilly Delores did lots of chores
And combined her weekend jobs
She delivered the papers
And walked the dog
That led to the shop
Where she mopped the floor
And baked the cakes
And made the snacks
That fattened the likes
Of Jack and his wife
Which drove the neighbours crazy

James and the Giant dress

(with a nod to Sea fever by John Masefield)

I must get out that dress again with the lovely seams and
    style.
And all I ask is the ballroom bar has beer to make me smile
and the meals quick, and the band is strong,
and my white veil will be shaking
and I'll sway there on the dance floor edge
to the music they are making.

I must get out that dress again for balls need a stunning
    bride.
And I'll stand tall and I'll stand proud and I will not be
    denied.
And all I ask is a windy day to blow my white train flying,
and a fun day in a fine room where someone else is buying.

I must get out that dress again and borrow it from the wife.
Cos while the galls away the males play and forget the
    stressful life.
And all I ask is some merry yarn and I'll wear the top
    crossed-over.
Then a quiet sleep and sweet dreams when the long long day
    is over.

Mother's ashes

We collected mother's ashes on a fine yet freezing day
and as we left the office the attendant he did say
'Be careful of those icy steps. It's mighty slippery there.
Unusually we're out of salt, so do take extra care.'
The steps were quite unpassable.
But we had to get away.
Then mother's voice came to my ear
and I did hear her say,
'Remember that I'm here for you!'
Just so, well that was it!
Cos suddenly I knew she was,
albeit shaped as grit.
So I scattered mothers ashes
on the crematorium stairs
and watched the ice melt clean away
on that crystal clear December day.

My favourite pens

Started with Bic then tried highlighter markers
Bright coloured biros then moved on to Parkers.
Got hooked on Paper-mate gel in the spring.
A cartridge felt good then a Quink filled syringe.

Fine liner Pentels for italic writing.
Refills and inkspills
and quills I delight in.
Free flowing rollerballed permanent pens.
These make great gifts for indelible freinds

Pens that write properly, with no inky splashes.
Felt-tips held close to my nose and eyelashes.
Fountains by Sheaffer that work without springs.
These are a few of my favourite things.

When the pen leaks
When the pens blue
When I've writer's cramp
I simply get hold of a firm Yard-O-Led
And then I don't feel so bad!

In September 2019, 432 'Nigels' ranging from seven months to 80 years old, from across the world , gathered at The Fleece Inn Worcestershire to 'celebrate Nigel-ness'. This poem is for all of them.

Nigels

The Nigels gathered, young and old
from everywhere around the world
to celebrate just being 'Nige'.
The Landlord happy to oblige.
'I'm a Nigel' he proudly boasted.
'This is the most in one room ever hosted'
There was even a little baby there.
Knee high Nigel, didn't care.
Nige the Great, enjoying fries,
Curly Nige and Nige the Wise.
It was Nigels Nigels everywhere
And all of them could drink.
A brilliant bunch of lovely fellas
including , of course, some fine Nigellas.
When XTC had played their song,
with plans for a Nigel of her own,
a lass went down on bended knee
saying 'Nigel...will you marry me?'
And all the Nigels held their breath
till Chosen Nigel...answered 'YES!'

Organ pipes

There's wind in the pipes of my organ.
And there's wind in the depths of my lungs.
I am sailing the wave of creation
with the breath of worlds life first begun.
All I own is this tiny harmonica
and these raggedy clothes on my back.
And my singing is desperately chronica
for refinement is something I lack.
So tie my torn shirt down sport
Oh tie my torn shirt down.
For the spirit of love is ascending
and I'm a sailor all salty and brown.
Though I pitch and I roll I go onwards.
Though the surface is strewn with debris.
All the rubbish is of my own making.
I have no-one to blame, only me.
Salt peppers the cheeks of the sailors
for our lives are discordant and coarse.
We sing shanties and sleep on the floor boards
and our snores are most gloriously hoarse.
Now there's creatures who swim in the water.
They are merfolk and horses with fins.
They are sirens all tempting and gorgeous
and we know we must never go in.
'Tis Beyond, this mystery we live for,
for Beyond is the place where we'll die .
'Ultreya !' the pilgrims cry 'Onwards!'
To the place where the sea meets the sky.

Poem of an Unsleeper

Is there no rest for me at all?
The sheep out-jump their number.
Oh give me please the peaceful breath,
untroubled sleep, and slumber.

'Lay your head upon the pillow
while the condensation forms
small beads of patterned moisture
on the windows of the dorms.
No worry will affect the course
of its inexorable drip.
So give yourself to sleep now
and into slumber slip.'

The soporific water slides
down the pane in streaks.
A rude awakening at once!
Cold splash upon my cheek!

But why, what for the cosmos
now does this? Forbids me sleep!
Cruel mantle of my fate! I'm bid
it's consciousness to keep.

Employees at a Swindon recruitment agency are being rewarded with four extra days of paid holiday for not smoking at work. The boss realised that a smoker who takes a ten minute smoking break three times a day is getting a lot of time out. The company decided to reward non-smokers with time off to balance things out. This inspired me to write this next poem.

Smoking guns

We are the Company smokers
and we enjoy our smoking break
and overall its plain to see
the difference that we make.
Though we struggle to climb ladders,
and don't progress up all the rungs,
in a way we have promoted YOU
by clogging up our lungs.
Now YOU can get four days off work.
Now YOU can get promoted.
It's a filthy job this smoking
but to YOU we are devoted.
Non-smokers, come, salute the fag.
The Union's colour's ochre.
And though we smell of nictotine
come, thank the Company smoker.
Other unions they have failed
in their talks with all the Biggies
to get you this much holiday
as we have with our ciggies.
When our addiction goes full time
then comes the Glorious Day.
For you will have it all in lieu
and still be on full pay.

An Australian man who lost his wallet in Melksham was delighted when a good Samaritan named Pete found it and mailed it back to him.

The tourist from Melbourne left his wallet on top of a rental car in August 2019 and drove off. He thought it was lost for good but six weeks later a package arrived at his home in Victoria. It contained his wallet and a note from 'Pete' saying he had found it by the side of the road in Melksham.

Strike me lucky!

'Wholly snappy ducks legs!' the Aussie tourist said.
Discovering the wallet gone, the shock went to his head.
'I've been a proper drongo and left it on the car.
Now I expect a yobbo's got it and has hoofed it to the bar.'
His normally smooth tanned forehead with worry it did
   pucker
as the sad distraught Australian borrowed lobsters for some
   tucker.
'I'm behaving like a pork chop but it really is quite hard
to find that you've lost all your cash and your Aussie credit
   card.'
When he returned to Wombat Crossing, another shock in
   store
for a parcel lay upon his mat inside his own front door.
'Well strike me lucky!' he exclaimed, as he bent to take a
   squiz
'I think this is me wallet. Struth . That is exactly what it is!'
He looked and found his cards intact, everything complete,
and a message with good wishes
that was simply signed 'from Pete'.

On the 13th December 2018 a Wiltshire auction house had a very unusual sale. Dozens of items belonging to the 1980s pop band Tears for Fears went under the hammer. The collection sold for nearly £40,000.

The band, formed in Bath by Roland Orzabal and Curt Smith, were famous for songs including Shout, Sowing the Seeds of Love and Mad World.

The memorabilia was all kit cleared from the garage of frontman Orzabal.

Tears for Fears auction

Job lot? Sob lot! Really damp!
There's a mesa boogie mark 3 amp.
Sequential circuits, overdrives.
Wait till the auctioneer arrives.
Tears for Fears are selling kit
so come on down and bid for it.
Most of it is fully wired,
though some of it's a little tired.
Marshall, Fender, loads of racks
Didn't they make lovely tracks?
There's Lexicon and Eventide,
with Hammond, Prophet side by side.
Transposers, super leads and more.
So come on. What are you waiting for?

The Doyouthinkhesaurus

We are the clever dinosaurs,
The Doyouthinkhesaurus.
We're massive but we're silent
till we burst out in loud chorus
'Way to go, tippy toe!'
and scare the daylights from you.
Once we sneaked into an ice cream shop.
Five lumbering Dinkysaurus!
And made the assistant drop the cones
when we burst out in loud chorus
'Way to go ,Creamy Joe!
We are the Dinkysaurs!'
And there was ice cream, ice cream, everywhere
and a raspberry ripple of applause.

The man that day-tripped worktops

My man, he leans on worktops.
They're the place he likes the best.
But he does not mix cakes or butter loaves.
He simply likes *to rest*.
He disrespects the workforce.
His yawning makes me sick.
Resting on a work surface!
That's... oxymoron-ic!
He leans and gazes at his own
reflection in the kettle.
But to actually flip the switch on?
Well it's clear he's got no mettle.
A worktop is for working on!
For sawing bread and roast,
for mixing jugs of gravy stock,
and sanding crumbs off toast.
There's drizzling, chopping, rolling.
There's kneading dough as well.
There's hand held gas fuelled
flame torches to scorch the caramel.
It's a place for *work* and using *tools*,
for culinary *graft*.
But he won't even lift a spoon
for things like sugar craft.
While I bustle all around him
he's at the counter keeping still.
It's like he thinks he's got a ticket
for a day in Lazyville.

In October 2018 KLEENEX announced the end of its 'Mansize'
brand following complaints to the company over sexism. ...
Kleenex for Men were first sold in 1956, with a claim that
the tissues would 'stay strong when wet'. The company said the
tissues would now simply be called 'Extra Large'. Some people in
Wiltshire mourned the loss of Mansize.

The end of man-size tissues

How can I dab his manly face
With my little hanky made of lace?
It could not absorb the tears he's shed.
It could not be knotted on his head.
I need a thing that is man size
If I'm to dry my old mans eyes